DRINKERS' VERSE

DRINKERS' VERSE

Brian Kellow and John Krisak

Hutchinson
London Melbourne Auckland Johannesburg

© Brian Kellow and John Krisak 1986

All rights reserved

This edition first published in 1986 by Hutchinson Ltd, an imprint of Century Hutchinson Ltd, Brookmount House, 62–65 Chandos Place, London, WC2N 4NW

Century Hutchinson Australia Pty Ltd,
PO Box 496, 16–22 Church Street, Hawthorn, Victoria 3122, Australia

Century Hutchinson New Zealand Ltd,
PO Box 40–086, Glenfield, Auckland 10, New Zealand

Century Hutchinson South Africa (Pty) Ltd,
PO Box 337, Bergvlei, 2012, South Africa

ISBN: 0 09 165951 5

Phototypeset in Linotron Times by
Input Typesetting Ltd, London.

Printed and bound in Great Britain
The Guernsey Press Co. Ltd., Guernsey, Channel Islands.

CONTENTS

Frontispiece

Top Fermented

Bottom Fermented

Vinted

Distilled

Alehouses

Alehouse Yarns

Drunkenness

ACKNOWLEDGEMENTS

Every reasonable effort has been made to trace the ownership of copyrighted material and to make due acknowledgement. Any errors or omissions will be gladly rectified in future editions.

The editors gratefully acknowledge permission to reproduce copyright poems in this book.

Hilaire Belloc: 'A Sussex Drinking Song'. Reprinted by permission of A. D. Peters & Company Ltd.

'Ballad of Liquid Refreshment' by E. C. Bentley. © E. C. Bentley. Reproduced by permission of Curtis Brown, London.

John Betjeman: 'The Arrest of Oscar Wilde At The Cadogan Hotel' from The Collected Poems of John Betjeman (John Murray Publishers). Reprinted by permission of John Murray Publishers, London.

G. K. Chesterton: 'The Logical Vegetarian', 'Wine and Water', 'The Rolling English Road', 'The Song of Right and Wrong', 'A Cider Song To J. S. M.', 'The Saracen's Head', 'The Englishman'. Reprinted by permission of Miss D. E. Collins.

'Interview With Doctor Drink' from The Collected Poems and Epigrams of J. V. Cunningham, Swallow Press, 1971. Reprinted with the permission of Ohio State University Press.

Robert Graves: 'Point of No Return' from Robert Graves: Collected Poems 1975. Reprinted with permission of the Executors of the Estate of Robert Graves.

Brian Higgins: 'A Corrupt Man in the French Pub' reprinted by permission of the author and Methuen, London.

'In a Prominent Bar in Secaucus One Day', reprinted from Cross Ties by X. J. Kennedy, Copyright © 1985 X. J. Kennedy. Reprinted by permission of the University of Georgia Press.

Patrick Lane: 'The Absinthe Drinker' from Beware The Months of Fire (Toronto: House of Anansi, 1974). Reprinted by permission of the author.

FRONTISPIECE

The Five Reasons

If all be true that I do think,
There are *Five Reasons* we should drink;
Good Wine, a Friend, or being Dry,
Or lest we should be by and by;
Or any other Reason why.

> *Henry Aldrich (1647–1710)*

TOP FERMENTED

The breasts of a barmaid

The breasts of a barmaid of Crale
Were tattooed with the price of brown ale,
  While on her behind
  For the sake of the blind
Was the same information in Braille.

Anonymous

The Good Wife's Ale

When shall we meet again, and have a taste
Of that transcendent Ale, we drank of last?
What wild ingredients did the Woman choose
To mad her drink with all; it made me lose
My wits before I quencht my thirst, there came
Such whimseys in my head, and such a flame
Of fiery drunkenness had singed my nose,
My beard shrunk in for fear. There were of those
That took me for a comet; some a far
Distance remote thought me a blazing star.
The Earth methought just as it was it went
Round in a wheeling course of merriment.
My head was ever drooping, and my nose

Offering to be a suitor to my toes.
My Mouth did stand awry just as it were
Lab'ring to whisper something in mine ear.
My pockholed face, they say, appeared to some
Most like a dry and burning honeycomb.
My tongue did swim in Ale, and joyed to boast
Himself a better seaman than the toast.
My guts were mines of sulphur, and my set
Of parched teeth struck fire as they met.
Nay, when I pist, my urine was so hot
It burnt a hole quite through the chamber-pot.
Each brewer that I met I kisst and made
Suitor to be apprentice to the trade.
One did approve the motion when he saw
That mine own legs did the indenture draw.
Well, Sir, I grew stark mad, as you may see
By this adventure upon poetry.
You easily may guess, I am not quite
Grown sober yet, by these poor lines I write.
I only do't for this, that you may see
That though you pay'd for th' Ale, yet it pay'd me.

Ben Jonson (1572–1637)

Wassail Song

We have been a walking
    Among the leaves so green,
And hither we are coming
    So stately to be seen.

With our wassel,
Our jolly wassel,
All joys come to you
And to our wassel bowl.

Good Master and good Mistress,
  As you sit by the fire,
Remember us poor wassellers
  That travel in the mire.

Our bowl is made
  Of the mulberry tree,
And so is your ale
  Of the best barley.

Pray rise up, master Butler,
  And put on your golden ring,
And bring to us a jug of ale,
  The better we shall sing.

Our purse it is made
  Of the finest calves skin,
We want a little silver
  To line it well within.

Good Master, good Mistress,
  If that you are but willing,
Send down two of your little boys
  To each of us a shilling.

We'll hang a silver napkin
  Upon a golden spear,
And come no more a wasselling
  Until another year.

Anonymous

Terence, This is Stupid Stuff

  'Terence, this is stupid stuff:
You eat your victuals fast enough;

There can't be much amiss, 'tis clear,
To see the rate you drink your beer.
But oh, good Lord, the verse you make,
It gives a chap the belly-ache.
The cow, the old cow, she is dead:
It sleeps well, the horned head:
We poor lads, 'tis our turn now
To hear such tunes as killed the cow.
Pretty friendship 'tis to rhyme
Your friends to death before their time
Moping melancholy mad:
Come, pipe a tune to dance to, lad.'

Why, if 'tis dancing you would be,
There's brisker pipes than poetry.
Say, for what were hop-yards meant,
Or why was Burton built on Trent?
Oh many a peer of England brews
Livelier liquor than the Muse,
And malt does more than Milton can
To justify God's ways to man.
Ale, man, ale's the stuff to drink
For fellows whom it hurts to think:
Look into the pewter pot
To see the world as the world's not.
And faith, 'tis pleasant till 'tis past:
The mischief is that 'twill not last.
Oh I have been to Ludlow fair
And left my necktie God knows where,
And carried half-way home, or near,
Pints and quarts of Ludlow beer.
Then the world seemed none so bad,
And I myself a sterling lad;
And down in lovely muck I've lain,
Happy till I woke again.
Then I saw the morning sky:
Heigho, the tale was all a lie:
The world, it was the old world yet,
I was I, my things were wet,
And nothing now remained to do
But begin the game anew.

Therefore, since the world has still
Much good, but much less good than ill,
And while the sun and moon endure
Luck's a chance, but trouble's sure
I'd face it as a wise man would,
And train for ill and not for good.
'Tis true, the stuff I bring for sale
Is not so brisk a brew as ale
Out of a stem that scored the hand
I wrung it in a weary land
But take it if the smack is sour,
The better for the embittered hour:
It should do good to heart and head
When your soul is in my soul's stead:
And I will friend you if I may,
In the dark and cloudy day.

There was a king reigned in the East:
There, when Kings will sit to feast,
They get their fill before they think
With poisoned meat and poisoned drink.
He gathered all that springs to birth
From the many-venomed earth:
First a little, thence to more,
He sampled all her killing store:
And easy, smiling, seasoned sound,
Sate the king when healths went round.
They put arsenic in his meat
And stared aghast to watch him eat;
They poured strychnine in his cup
And shook to see him drink it up:
They shook, they stared as white's their shirt:
Them it was their poison hurt.
–I tell the tale that I heard told.
Mithridates, he died old.

A. E. Housman (1859–1936)

6

A Sussex Drinking Song

On Sussex hills where I was bred,
When lanes in autumn rains are red,
When Arun tumbles in his bed,
  And busy great gusts go by;
When branch is bare in Burton Glen
And Bury Hill is a whitening, then,
I drink strong ale with gentlemen;
  Which nobody can deny, deny,
    Deny, deny, deny, deny,
      Which nobody can deny!

In half-November off I go,
To push my face against the snow,
And watch the winds wherever they blow
  Because my heart is high:
Till I settle me down in Steyning to sing
Of the women I met in my wandering,
And of all that I mean to do in the spring
  Which nobody can deny, deny,
    Deny, deny, deny, deny,
      Which nobody can deny!

Then times be rude and weather be rough
And ways be foul and fortune tough,
We are of the stout South Country stuff,
That never can have good ale enough,
  And do this chorus cry!
From Crowboro' Top to Ditchling Down,
From Hurstpierpoint to Arundel town,
The girls are plump and the ale is brown:
  Which nobody can deny, deny,
    Deny, deny, deny, deny!
      If he does he tells a lie!

Hilaire Belloc (1870–1953)

The Englishman

St George he was for England,
And before he killed the dragon
He drank a pint of English ale
Out of an English flagon.
For though he fast right readily
In hair-shirt or in mail,
It isn't safe to give him cakes
Unless you give him ale.

St George he was for England,
And right gallantly set free
The lady left for dragon's meat
And tied up to a tree;
But since he stood for England
And knew what England means,
Unless you give him bacon
You mustn't give him beans.

St George he is for England,
And shall wear the shield he wore
When we go out in armour
With the battle-cross before.
But though he is jolly company
And very pleased to dine,
It isn't safe to give him nuts
Unless you give him wine.

G. K. Chesterton (1874–1936)

On Gabriel Richardson

Here brewer Gabriel's fire's extinct,
    And empty all his barrels:

He's blest—if as he brew'd he drink—
   In upright, honest morals.

                    Robert Burns (1759–1796)

At night

At night when ale is in,
   Like friends we part to bed;
In morrow grey, when ale is out,
   Then hatred is in head.

                         Anonymous

BOTTOM FERMENTED

Prohibition

prohibition makes you
want to cry
into your beer and
denies you the beer
to cry into

Don Marquis (1878–1937)

I Likes a Drop of Good Beer

Come one and all, both great and small,
With voices loud and clear,
And let us sing, bless Billy the King,
Who bated the tax upon beer.

> *Chorus.*
> *For I likes a drop of good beer, I does,*
> *I'se pertickler fond of my beer, I is,*
> *And — his eyes, whoever he tries*
> *To rob a poor man of his beer.*

Let Ministers shape the Duty on Cape,
And cause Port wine to be dear,

So that they keep, the bread and meat cheap,
And gie us a drop of good beer.

In drinking of rum, the maggots will come,
And soon bald pates will appear;
I never goes out, but I carries about,
My little pint noggin of beer.

My wife and I, feel always dry,
At market on Saturday night,
Then a noggin of beer, I never need fear,
For my wife always says it is right.

In harvest field, there's nothing can yield,
The labouring man such good cheer,
To reap and sow, and make barley grow,
And to give them a skinfull of beer.

The farmer's board will plenty afford,
Let it come from far, or from near,
And at harvest home, the jug will foam,
If he gives his men plenty of beer.

Long may Queen Victoria reign,
And be to her subjects dear,
And we'll wallop her foes, wherever we goes,
Only give us a skinfull of beer.

Anonymous

Under the Anheuser Bush

Talk about the shade of the sheltering palms,
Praise the bamboo tree and its wide spreading charms,
There's a little bush that grows right here in town,
You know its name, it has won such renown:

Often with my sweetheart just after the play,
To this little place then my footsteps will stray,
If she hesitates when she looks at the sign,
Softly I whisper, 'Now Sue don't decline.'

> *Come, Come, Come and make eyes with me,*
> *Under the Anheuser Bush.*
> *Come, Come, drink some 'Budwise' with me*
> *Under the Anheuser Bush,*
> *Hear the old German band,*
> *Just let me hold your hand, Yah!*
> *Do, Do, Come and have a stein or two,*
> *Under the Anheuser Bush.*

Rave about the place where your swells go to dine,
Picture Sue and me with our sandwich and stein,
Underneath the bush where the good fellows meet,
Life seems worth living, our joy is complete.
If you're sad at heart, take a trip there tonight,
You'll forget your woe and your eyes will grow bright,
There you'll surely find me with my sweetheart Sue,
Come down this ev'ning, I'll introduce you.

Andrew B. Sterling (1874–1955)

Bacchanal

You there, and you, and you
Come, I want to embrace you
With beer on your breath and halitosis
Come with your Venus-rotted noses

Here is man's true temple, cool
Gloom, sincere worshippers—
Before them the tapers of beer
Like lights lit on many altars

Come, pleasure's my god and yours
Too, to go by your charming noises
Let's hiccup our happiness
And belch our ecstasies to Bacchus

He hears us and sends the room
Spinning. May his touch be always upon us.
May we, as he spins us in the cool gloom,
Be forever in his keeping.

Irving Layton (1912–   )

West Sussex Drinking Song

They sell good Beer at Haslemere
    And under Guildford Hill.
At Little Cowfold as I've been told,
    A beggar may drink his fill:
There is a good brew in Amberley too,
    And by the bridge also;
But the swipes they take in at Washington Inn
    Is the very best Beer I know.

Chorus
    With my here it goes, there it goes,
        All the fun's before us:
    The Tipple's Aboard and the night is young,
    The door's ajar and the Barrel is sprung,
    I am singing the best song ever was sung
        And it has a rousing chorus.

If I were what I never can be,
    The master or the squire:
If you gave me the hundred from here to the sea,
    Which is more than I desire:
Then all my crops should be barley and hops,

And did my harvest fail
I'd sell every rood of mine acres I would
  For a belly-full of good Ale.

        Chorus
  With my here it goes, there it goes,
    All the fun's before us:
  The Tipple's aboard and the night is young,
  The door's ajar and the Barrel is sprung,
  I am singing the best song ever was sung
    And it has a rousing Chorus.

                Hilaire Belloc (1870–1953)

Young Man of Porthcawl

There was a young man of Porthcawl
Who thought he was Samson or Saul:
These thoughts so obscure
Were due to the brewer,
And not to his ego at all.

        A. G. Prys-Jones (1888–   )

Idyll

Hermit hoar, in solemn cell,
  Wearing out life's evening grey,
Strike thy bosom, Sage, and tell
  What is bliss, and which the way.

Thus I spoke, and speaking sighed,
  Scarce repressed the starting tear,
When the hoary sage replied,
  'Come, my lad, and drink some beer.'

Samuel Johnson (1709–1784)

Come, Landlord, Fill the Flowing Bowl

Come, landlord, fill the flowing bowl
  Until it doth run over;
For to-night we'll merry merry be,
  To-morrow we'll be sober.

The man who drinketh small beer
  And goes to bed quite sober,
Fades as the leaves do fade
  That drop off in October.

But he who drinks just what he likes
  And getteth half-seas over,
Will live until he dies perhaps,
  And then lie down in clover.

The man who kisses a pretty girl
  And goes and tells his mother,
Ought to have his lips cut off,
  And never kiss another.

Anonymous

VINTED

The rapture

The rapture of drinking
And wine's dizzy joy
No man who is sober deserves.

Li Po (701–762)

A Drinking Song

Come, thou monarch of the vine,
Plumpy Bacchus, with pink eyne!
In thy fats our cares be drowned,
With thy grapes our hairs be crowned.
  Cup us, till the world go round,
  Cup us, till the world go round!

William Shakespeare (1564–1616)

Corkscrew Carol

Blest bright names of Burgundy,
Light the candles on my tree.

Meursault, Chablis, Chambertin,
Raise in me the Christmas man.

Raise in me love dead and gone
Pommard, Beaujolais and Beaune.

Ashes crowned, with cloth of sack on,
Let me now rejoice in Macon.

I'll rejoice and hang the holly,
Hang expense and melancholy.

Hang your bright Burgundian names
Round the tree in bottled flames.

Holy Night and *nuit si jolie*,
Nuits St. George and sweet Vin Volnay . . .

Laurie Lee (1914–   )

Ballade Beaune

There are merits in whisky and stout;
Of rum I am no deprecator;
And gin is a blessing, no doubt,
To those who live near the Equator;
In Russia, with vodka they cater
For warmth in that boreal zone:
But Burgundy's cleaner and straighter,
Bring me a bottle of Beaune!

Champagne one is better without,
While Schnapps as a drink's a third-rater;
Liqueurs cause laryngeal drought,
A thirst like Vesuvius' crater:
Of Malmsey and Sack I lack data,

17

They may have a charm of their own,
But (if I'm to be a debater)
Bring me a bottle of Beaune!

Port is productive of gout,
And brandy makes many a prater;
Think of (with feelings devout)
The hooch that is made from the 'tater;
So let us thank the Creator
Who ripens the grapes by the Rhône,
For Burgundy's never a traitor,
Bring me a bottle of Beaune!

     Prince, I'll attend to you later,
  Or give you a call on the 'phone,
    I'm busy at present . . .
         'Hi! Waiter!
  Bring me a bottle of Beaune!'

H. S. Mackintosh

Drinking Song

On the Excellence of Burgundy Wine

My jolly fat host with your face all a-grin,
Come, open the door to us, let us come in.
A score of stout fellows who think it no sin
If they toast till they're hoarse, and they drink till they spin,
    Hoofed it amain,
    Rain or no rain,
  To crack your old jokes, and your bottle to drain.

Such a warmth in the belly that nectar begets
As soon as his guts with its humour he wets,
The miser his gold, and the student his debts,

And the beggar his rags and his hunger forgets.
    For there's never a wine
    Like this tipple of thine
  From the great hill of Nuits to the River of Rhine.

Outside you may hear the great gusts as they go
By Foy, by Duerne, and the hills of Lerraulx,
But the rain he may rain, and the wind he may blow,
If the Devil's above there's good liquor below.
    So it abound,
    Pass it around,
  Burgundy's Burgundy all the year round.

Hilaire Belloc (1870–1953)

My Bony Mary

Go fetch to me a pint o' wine,
  And fill it in a silver tassie;
That I may drink, before I go,
  A service to my bonie lassie:
The boat rocks at the Pier o' Lieth.
  Fu' loud the wind blaws frae the Ferry,
The ship rides by the Berwick-law,
  And I maun leave my bony Mary.

The trumpets sound, the banners fly,
  The glittering spears are ranked ready,
The shouts o' war are heard afar,
  The battle closes deep and bloody.
It's not the toar o' sea or shore,
  Wad make me langer wish to tarry;
Nor shouts o' war that's heard afar–
  It's leaving thee, my bony Mary!

Robert Burns (1759–1796)

19

The dew

The dew is heavy on the grass,
At last the sun is set.
Fill up, fill up the cup of jade
The night's before us yet.

Anonymous

Drinking Wine

Confucian scholars love strange antiquity,
No sooner open their mouth than gab about Yao and Shun.
If they were born before the time of Fu-hsi,
What'd have been the topic of their discourse?
Now the ancients have all passed away,
And their ways are found in what they left behind.
But since not a single word in them can be made good,
Ten thousand volumes are all useless things.
So I wish only to drink my wine,
And not to know the rest.
Look, the people in the Land of the Happy-drunk
Lived long before Heaven and earth began.

Lin Hung (Fourteenth Century)
trans. Irving Y. Lo

Drinking Wine

The world is full of those who love to be officials,
Never again can they savor the sweet taste of wine.

There are also those who love wine,
They have no time to ponder how good it is to be an official.
Love of wine makes people wild,
Love of official life turns them base.
Even when his insides rot, a drinker won't quit drinking;
In the wee hours of the night, an official won't stop working.
To be fond of wine or to crave for titles,
Each in its own way can cause death.

I have always loved being an official,
A junior secretary wasn't too lowly for me.
But I'm also among those who love wine,
My cellar is always full.
This year my luck runs afoul–
Dismissed from office, I didn't do well with wine either.
With a long sigh, I say goodby to the capital:
I know it's time to pack up and leave!

Anonymous
trans. Irving Y. Lo

Drinking Alone Beneath the Moon

A pot of wine among the flowers:
I drink alone, no kith or kin near.
I raise my cup to invite the moon to join me;
It and my shadow make a party of three.
Alas, the moon is unconcerned about drinking,
And my shadow merely follows me around.
Briefly I cavort with the moon and my shadow:
Pleasure must be sought while it is spring.
I sing and the moon goes back and forth,
I dance and my shadow falls at random.
While sober we seek pleasure in fellowship;
When drunk we go each our own way.

Then let us pledge a friendship without human ties
And meet again at the far end of the Milky Way.

Li Po (701–762)

Drunk Too Soon

Today before a goblet of wine I was shamed,
My third cup unfinished, I couldn't pour another.
Wondering why I am always drunk beneath the flowers,
Perhaps the spring breeze has made me tipsy.

Yuan Ch'en (779–831)
trans. Dell R. Hales

From Tancred
[Act 1, Sc. i]
Song

The peasant sun went crushing grapes,
Purple and gold along the road,
Where sylvan gods and antique shapes
Bear up the vine the clusters load.

Rock-hewn and grey the mountain towns
Throbbed into gold as he drew near;
Glowed with the fruit the vine-leaf crowns,
Over the doorways hanging clear.

His rustic face was lit with fire,
This lover of the Latin vine,
His Southern eyes burned with desire,
Before the wine-jars waiting wine.

Over old walls the clusters hung,
As he went crushing grapes content;
I felt the song he should have sung,
And thrilled with leafy merriment.

Laurence Dakin (1904–   )

Drinking Song

She tells me with claret she cannot agree,
And she thinks of a hogshead whene'er she sees me;
For I smell like a beast, and therefore must I
Resolve to forsake her, or claret deny.
Must I leave my dear bottle, that was always my friend,
And I hope will continue so to my life's end?
Must I leave it for her? 'Tis a very hard task:
Let her go to the devil!—bring the other full flask.

Had she taxed me with gaming, and bid me forbear,
'Tis a thousand to one I had lent her an ear:
Had she found out my Sally, up three pair of stairs,
I had balked her, and gone to St. James's to prayers.
Had she bade me read homilies three times a day,
She perhaps had been humoured with little to say;
But, at night, to deny me my bottle of red,
Let her go to the devil!—there's no more to be said.

Anonymous

A Drinking-Song

Bacchus must now his power resign—
I am the only God of Wine!

23

It is not fit the wretch should be
In competition set with me,
Who can drink ten times more than he.

Make a new world, ye powers divine!
Stock'd with nothing else but Wine:
Let Wine its only product be,
Let Wine be earth, and air, and sea—
And let that Wine be all for me!

Henry Carey (1687–1743)

Drinking Song

There are people, I know, to be found,
  Who say, and apparently think,
That sorrow and care may be drowned
  By a timely consumption of drink.

Does not man, these enthusiasts ask,
  Most nearly approach the divine,
When engaged in the soul-stirring task
  Of filling his body with wine?

Have not beggars been frequently known,
  When satisfied, soaked and replete,
To imagine their bench was a throne
  And the civilised world at their feet?

Lord Byron has finely described
  The remarkably soothing effect
Of liquor, profusely imbibed,
  On a soul that is shattered and wrecked.

In short, if your body or mind
  Or your soul or your purse come to grief,

You need only get drunk, and you'll find
   Complete and immediate relief.

For myself, I have managed to do
   Without having recourse to this plan,
So I can't write a poem for you,
   And you'd better get someone who can.

              J. K. Stephen (1859–1892)

Ballade of Liquid Refreshment

Last night we started with some dry vermouth;
   Some ancient sherry with a golden glow;
Then many flagons of the soul of fruit
   Such as Burgundian vineyards only grow;
   A bottle each of port was not *de trop*;
And then old brandy till the east was pink
   —But talking makes me hoarse as any crow.
Excuse me while I go and have a drink.

Some talk of Alexander: some impute
   Absorbency to Mirabeau-Tonneau;
Some say that General Grant and King Canute,
   Falstaff and Pitt and Edgar Allan Poe,
   Prince Charlie, Carteret, Hans Breitmann—so
The list goes on—they say that these could clink
   The can, and take their liquor—*A propos!*
Excuse me while I go and have a drink.

Spirit of all that lives, from God to brute,
   Spirit of love and life, of sun and snow,
Spirit of leaf and limb, of race and root,
   How wonderfully art thou prison'd! Lo!
   I quaff the cup, I feel the magic flow,
And Superman succeeds to Missing Link,

(I say, 'I quaff'; but am I quaffing? No!
Excuse me while I go and have a drink.)

Envoi

Hallo there, Prince! Is that you down below
Kicking and frying by the brimstone brink?
    Well, well! It had to come some time, you know.
Excuse me while I go and have a drink.

E. C. Bentley (1875–1956)

Stanza: A Fragment

I would to heaven that I were so much clay
    As I am blood, bone, marrow, passion, feeling—
For then at least the past were pass'd away—
    And for the future—(but I write this reeling,
Having got drunk exceedingly today,
    So that I seem to stand upon the ceiling)
I say—the future is a serious matter—
And so—for God's sake—hock and soda-water!

Lord Byron (1788–1824)

Fill the Goblet Again

Fill the goblet again! for I never before
Felt the glow that now gladdens my heart to its core;
Let us drink!—who would not?—since through life's varied
    round
In the goblet alone no deception is found.

I have tried in its turn all that life can supply;
I have basked in the beam of a dark rolling eye;
I have loved!—who has not?—but what heart can declare,
That pleasure existed whilst passion was there?

In the bright days of youth, when the heart's in its spring,
And dreams that affection can never take wing,
I had friends!—who has not?—but what tongue will avow,
That friends, rosy wine, are so faithful as thou?

The heart of a mistress some boy may estrange;
Friendship shifts with the sunbeam—thou never canst change,
Thou grow'st old!—who does not?—but on earth what
    appears,
Whose virtues, like thine, still increase with its years?

Yet if blest to the utmost that love can bestow,
Should a rival bow down to our idol below,
We are jealous—who's not?—thou hast no such alloy;
For the more that enjoy thee, the more they enjoy.

Lord Byron (1788–1824)

With an Honest Old Friend

With an honest old friend and a merry old song,
And a flask of old port let me sit the night long,
And laugh at the malice of those who repine
That they must drink porter whilst I can drink wine.

I envy no mortal though ever so great,
Nor scorn I a wretch for his lowly estate;
But what I abhor and esteem as a curse,
Is poorness of spirit, not poorness of purse.

Then dare to be generous, dauntless and gay,
Let us merrily pass life's remainder away;
Upheld by our friends, we our foes may despise,
For the more we are envied, the higher we rise.

Henry Carey (1687–1743)

Non sum qualis eram bonae sub regno Cynarae

Last night, ah, yesternight, betwixt her lips and mine
There fell thy shadow, Cynara! thy breath was shed
Upon my soul between the kisses and the wine;
And I was desolate and sick of an old passion,
    Yea, I was desolate and bow'd my head:
I have been faithful to thee, Cynara! in my fashion.

All night upon mine heart I felt her warm heart beat,
Night-long within mine arms in love and sleep she lay;
Surely the kisses of her bought red mouth were sweet;
But I was desolate and sick of an old passion,
    When I awoke and found the dawn was gray:
I have been faithful to thee, Cynara! in my fashion.

I have forgot much, Cynara! gone with the wind,
Flung roses, roses, riotously with the throng,
Dancing, to put thy pale lost lilies out of mind;
But I was desolate and sick of an old passion,
    Yea, all the time, because the dance was long:
I have been faithful to thee, Cynara! in my fashion.

I cried for madder music and for stronger wine,
But when the feast is finish'd and the lamps expire,
Then falls thy shadow, Cynara! the night is thine;

And I am desolate and sick of an old passion,
    Yea, hungry for the lips of my desire:
I have been faithful to thee, Cynara! in my fashion.

Ernest Dowson (1867–1900)

Vitae summa brevis spem nos vetat incohare longam

They are not long, the weeping and the laughter,
    Love and desire and hate:
I think they have no portion in us after
        We pass the gate.

They are not long, the days of wine and roses:
    Out of a misty dream
Our path emerges for a while, then closes
        Within a dream.

Ernest Dowson (1867–1900)

The Song of Right and Wrong

Feast on wine or fast on water
And your honour shall stand sure,
God Almighty's son and daughter
He the valiant, she the pure;
If an angel out of heaven
Brings you other things to drink,
Thank him for his kind attentions,
Go and pour them down the sink.

Tea is like the East he grows in,
A great yellow Mandarin
With urbanity of manner
And unconsciousness of sin;
All the women, like a harem,
At his pig-tail troop along;
And, like all the East he grows in,
He is Poison when he's strong.

Tea, although an Oriental,
Is a gentleman at least;
Cocoa is a cad and coward,
Cocoa is a vulgar beast,
Cocoa is a dull, disloyal,
Lying, crawling cad and clown,
And may very well be grateful
To the fool that takes him down.

As for all the windy waters,
They were rained like tempests down
When good drink had been dishonoured
By the tipplers of the town;
When red wine had brought red ruin
And the death-dance of our times,
Heaven sent us Soda Water
As a torment for our crimes.

G. K. Chesterton (1874–1936)

A Serving Men's Song

Granichus. O! for a bowl of fat Canary,
　　　　　 Rich Palermo, sparkling Sherry,
　　　　　 Some nectar else, from Juno's dairy;
　　　　　 O! these draughts would make us merry.

Psyllus.	O! for a wench (I deal in faces,
	And in other daintier things);
	Tickled am I with her embraces.
	Fine dancing in such fairy rings.

Manes.	O! for a plump fat leg of mutton,
	Veal, lamb, capon, pig, and coney:
	None is happy but a glutton,
	None an ass but who wants money.

Chorus.	Wines (indeed) and girls are good,
	But brave victuals feast the blood;
	For wenches, wine, and lusty cheer,
	Jove would leap down to surfeit here.

John Lyly (1554–1606)

The praise of Bacchus

The praise of Bacchus then the sweet musician sung,
Of Bacchus ever fair and ever young:
  The jolly god in triumph comes;
  Sound the trumpets; beat the drums;
    Flushed with a purple grace
    He shows his honest face:
Now give the hautboys breath; he comes, he comes,

Bacchus ever fair and young
  Drinking joys did first ordain;
Bacchus' blessings are a treasure;
  Drinking is the soldier's pleasure;
    Rich the treasure;
    Sweet the pleasure;
Sweet is pleasure after pain.

John Dryden (1631–1700)

31

Wine and Water

Old Noah he had an ostrich farm and fowls on the largest
    scale,
He ate his egg with a ladle in an egg-cup big as a pail,
And the soup he took was Elephant Soup and the fish he took
    was Whale,
But they all were small to the cellar he took when he set out
    to sail,
And Noah he often said to his wife when he sat down to dine,
'I don't care where the water goes if it doesn't get into the
    wine.'

The cataract of the cliff of heaven fell blinding off the brink
As if it would wash the stars away as suds go down a sink,
The seven heavens came roaring down for the throats of hell
    to drink,
And Noah he cocked his eye and said, 'It looks like rain, I
    think.
The water has drowned the Matterhorn as deep as a Mendip
    mine,
But I don't care where the water goes if it doesn't get into
    the wine.'

But Noah he sinned, and we have sinned; on tipsy feet we
    trod,
Till a great big black teetotaller was sent for us for a rod,
And you can't get wine at a P.S.A., or chapel, or Eisteddfod,
For the Curse of Water has come again because of the wrath
    of God,
And water is on the Bishop's board and the Higher Thinker's
    shrine,
But I don't care where the water goes if it doesn't get into
    the wine.

G. K. Chesterton (1874–1936)

Boy serving

Boy serving out our good old friend
Falernian, give me a stronger blend.
Postumia says so—and the right
To rule the revelry tonight
Belongs to her (look, she's as tight
As the juice in a grapeskin!). Oh, I can't bear
You, water, wine-killer. Run elsewhere,
Find a new home with prudes. With us
The wine is pure Thyonius.

Catullus (1884–1954)

DISTILLED

Reflexions on Ice-Breaking

Candy
is dandy
But liquor
is quicker.

Ogden Nash (1902–1971)

A bumper of good liquor

A bumper of good liquor
Will end a contest quicker
Than justice, judge, or vicar.

Richard Brinsley Sheridan (1751–1816)

A sovereign drink

A sovereign drink—the chroniclers declare
If it be taken orderlie—beware

Of surfeit. Sip it and you'll find
It sloweth age and brighteneth the mind.
It keepeth head from whirling, teeth from chattering,
Tongue from lisping and throat from rattling.
It keepeth heart from swelling, guts from rumbling.
The hands from shivering and the bones from crumbling.

Theoricus (Thirteenth Century)

If ever I marry

If ever I marry a wife,
   I'll marry a landlord's daughter,
For then I may sit in the bar,
   And drink cold brandy and water.

Charles Lamb (1775–1834)

From the Bathing Machine Came a Din

From the bathing machine came a din
As of jollification within;
   It was heard far and wide,
   And the incoming tide
Had a definite flavour of gin.

Edward Gorey (1925–   )

Willie brew'd a peck o' maut

O Willie brew'd a peck o' maut,
   And Rob and Allan cam to see;
Three blyther hearts, that lee lang night,
   Ye wad na found in Christendie.

Chorus
We are na fou, we're nae that fou,
   But just a drappie in our e'e;
The cock may craw, the day may daw,
   And ay we'll taste the barley bree.

Here are we met, three merry boys,
   Three merry boys I trow are we;
And mony a night we've merry been,
   And mony mae we hope to be!
     Cho: We are na fou, &c.

It is the moon, I ken her horn,
   That's blinkin in the lift sae hie;
She shines sae bright to wyle us hame,
   But by my sooth she'll wait a wee!
     Cho: We are na fou, &c.

Wha first shall rise to gang awa,
   A cuckold, coward loun is he!
Wha first beside his chair shall fa',
   He is the king amang us three!
     Cho: We are na fou, &c.

Robert Burns (1759–1796)

Heather Ale
A Galloway Legend

From the bonny bells of heather
   They brewed a drink long-syne,

Was sweeter far than honey,
   Was stronger far than wine.
They brewed it and they drank it,
   And lay in a blessed swound
For days and days together
   In their dwellings underground.

There rose a king in Scotland,
   A fell man to his foes,
He smote the Picts in battle,
   He hunted them like roes.
Over miles of the red mountain
   He hunted as they fled,
And strewed the dwarfish bodies
   Of the dying and the dead.

Summer came in the country,
   Red was the heather bell;
But the manner of the brewing
   Was none alive to tell.
In graves that were like children's
   On many a mountain head,
   The Brewsters of the Heather
   Lay numbered with the dead.

The king in the red moorland
   Rode on a summer's day;
And the bees hummed, and the curlews
   Cried beside the way.
The king rode, and was angry,
   Black was his brow and pale,
To rule in a land of heather
   And lack the Heather Ale.

It fortuned that his vassals,
   Riding free on the heath,
Came on a stone that was fallen
   And vermin hid beneath.
Rudely plucked from their hiding,
   Never a word they spoke:

A son and his aged father–
  Last of the dwarfish folk.

The king sat high on his charger,
  He looked on the little men;
And the dwarfish and swarthy couple
  Looked at the king again.
Down by the shore he had them;
  And there on the giddy brink–
'I will give you life, ye vermin,
  For the secret of the drink.'

There stood the son and father
  And they looked high and low;
The heather was red around them
  The sea rumbled below.
And up and spoke the father,
  Shrill was his voice to hear:
'I have a word in private,
  A word for the royal ear.

'Life is dear to the agèd,
  And honour a little thing;
I would gladly sell the secret,'
  Quoth the Pict to the King.
His voice was small as a sparrow's,
  And shrill and wonderful clear:
'I would gladly sell my secret,
  Only my son I fear.

'For life is a little matter,
  And death is nought to the young;
And I dare not sell my honour
  Under the eye of my son.
Take *him*, O king, and bind him,
  And cast him far in the deep;
And it's I will tell the secret
  That I have sworn to keep.'

They took the son and bound him,
  Neck and heels in a thong,

And a lad took him and swung him,
  And flung him far and strong,
And the sea swallowed his body,
  Like that of a child of ten;–
And there on the cliff stood the father,
  Last of the dwarfish men.

'True was the word I told you:
  Only my son I feared;
For I doubt the sapling courage
  That goes without the beard.
But now in vain is the torture,
  Fire shall never avail:
Here dies in my bosom
  The secret of Heather Ale.'

R. L. Stevenson (1850–1894)

My Papa's Waltz

The whiskey on your breath
Could make a small boy dizzy;
But I hung on like death:
Such waltzing was not easy.

We romped until the pans
Slid from the kitchen shelf;
My mother's countenance
Could not unfrown itself.

The hand that held my wrist
Was battered on one knuckle;
At every step you missed
My right ear scraped a buckle.

You beat time on my head
With a palm caked hard by dirt,

Then waltzed me off to bed
Still clinging to your shirt.

Theodore Roethke
(1908–1963)

Drink

My whiskey is
a tough way of life:

The wild cherry
continually pressing back
peach orchards.

I am a penniless
rumsoak.

Where shall I have that solidity
which trees find
in the ground?

My stuff
is the feel of good legs
and a broad pelvis
under the gold hair ornaments
of skyscrapers.

William Carlos Williams
(1883–1963)

the demon rum

well boss on these
rainy days i wish i was
web footed like a jersey mosquito no
one has yet invented
an umbrella for cockroaches i was
over across the street
to the barroom you used to
frequent before you reformed today
and it was raining outside i
pulled a piece of cheese
rind over my head to
protect me from the weather and
started for the door as i
passed by one of the booths a man
who was sitting in it said to
his companions please call a
taxi for me where do you want to go
said his companion i am
bad again said the man i want to
go to some place where they
treat nervous diseases
at once you look all right
said his companion i may look all
right said he but i don t see
all right i just saw a piece
of cheese rind crawling along the
floor and as i passed by i
said to myself beware the demon rum
it gives your brain a quirk
it puts you on the bum
and gives the doctors work

archy

Don Marquis (1878–1937)

The Little Brown Jug

My wife and I live all alone,
In a little hut we call our own,
She loves gin and I love rum,
Tell you what it is, don't we have fun?

Ha, ha, ha! 'Tis you and me,
Little brown jug, don't I love thee?
Ha, ha, ha! 'Tis you and me,
Little brown jug, don't I love thee?

If I had a cow that gave such beer,
I'd dress her in the finest sheer,
Feed her on the choicest hay,
And milk her twenty times a day.

'Tis gin that makes my friends my foes,
'Tis gin that makes me wear old clothes,
But seeing you are so near my nose,
Tip her up and down she goes.

When I go toiling on my farm,
Take little brown jug under my arm,
Set it under some shady tree,
Little brown jug, don't I love thee?

Then came the landlord tripping in,
Round top hat and a peaked chin,
In his hand he carried a cup,
Says I, 'Old fellow, give us a sup.'

If all the folks in Adam's race
Were put together in one place,
Then I'd prepare to drop a tear
Before I'd part with you, my dear.

Anonymous

The Lacquer Liquor Locker

Now once upon a time the King of Astrakhan, at that,
Was sitting on his throne because his throne was where he
        sat;
And comfortably beside him, and magnificently stocked,
Was a lacquer liquor locker which a liquor lackey locked.

'My boy,' the King would often say with granulated voice,
'I think the 1640 is particularly choice.'
The boy would understand and so, endeavoring to please,
He'd try his luck at fitting several likely locker keys.

The King was always much annoyed because of this delay:
'See here, my lad, you've got to throw those other keys away.'
'This minute, Sire?' 'This minute, sir!' And with a pox that
        pocked,
He cursed the keys which didn't keep his liquor locker locked.

The lackey did as he was bid. Alackalasalack!
He threw them all so far away that no one threw them back
A silly throw, as I can show, for he was simply shocked
To find he lacked the very one that left the liquor locked.

'O Sire, I've thrown them all away!' 'Look here, my liquor
        lad!'
'It so befell I threw as well the one I wish I had.'
And since it was the kind of lock that isn't quickly picked,
The lacquer liquid locker had the little lackey licked.

Unhappy page! In such a rage a king is hard to calm;
A butt or tun of '51's the proper kind of balm.
'I always liked my liquor locked, from brandy down to beer;
It might as well be lacquer now as liquor under here.'

Not magic of the magi nor the wisdom of the wise
Could either find the key again or ply where it applies.
The stricken King of Astrakhan soon sickened unto death,
Who tasted not of bitters but what most embittereth.

The little lackey lastly fell into a deep decline,
And evil over all the land to shrivel up the vine:
And now the only vintages of Astrakhan are crocked
In that lacquer liquor locker which a liquor lackey locked.

David McCord (1897–   )

In Obitum Promi

That Death should thus from hence our Butler catch,
Into my mind it cannot quickly sink;
Sure Death came thirsty to the Buttery Hatch
When he (that busy was) denied him drink.

Tut, 'twas not so; 'tis like he gave him liquor,
And Death, made drunk, took him away the quicker–
   Yet let not others grieve too much in mind,
    (The Butler gone) the keys are left behind.

Henry Parrot

John Barley-Corn, My Foe

John Barley-Corn, my foe, John,
   The song I have to sing
Is not in praise of you, John
   E'en though you are a king.
Your subjects they are legion, John,
   I find where'er I go:
They wear your yoke upon their necks,
   John Barley-Corn, my foe.

John Barley-Corn, my foe, John,
　By your despotic sway
The people of our country, John,
　Are suffering to-day.
You lay the lash upon their backs:
　Yet willingly they go
And pay allegiance at the polls,
　John Barley-Corn, my foe.

John Barley-Corn, my foe, John,
　You've broken many a heart,
And caused the bitter tear, John,
　From many an eye to start,
The widow and the fatherless
　From pleasant homes to go,
And lead a life of sin and shame,
　John Barley-Corn, my foe.

John Barley-Corn, my foe, John,
　May Heaven speed the hour,
When Temperance shall wear the crown
　And Rum shall lose its power;
When from the East unto the West
　the people all shall know
Their greatest curse has been removed,
　John Barley-Corn, my foe!

Charles Follen Adams (1842–1918)

ALEHOUSES

The Little Vagabond

Dear Mother, dear Mother, the Church is cold,
But the Ale-house is healthy & pleasant & warm;
Besides I can tell where I am used well,
Such usage in Heaven will never do well.

But if at the Church they would give us some Ale,
And a pleasant fire our souls to regale,
We'd sing and we'd pray all the live-long day,
Nor ever once wish from the Church to stray.

Then the Parson might preach, & drink & sing,
And we'd be as happy as birds in the spring;
And modest Dame Lurch, who is always at Church,
Would not have bandy children, nor fasting, nor birch.

And God, like a father rejoicing to see
His children as pleasant and happy as he,
Would have no more quarrel with the Devil or the Barrel,
But kiss him, & give him both drink and apparel.

William Blake (1757–1827)

At the Ship

The firelight flickered on the age-old beams
As I sat drinking in the taproom of the Ship;

From some far-distant room I heard the sound of screams.
　　I poked the fire and took another sip.

　　The barman came and leaned upon the bar,
Rubbing his fulgent nose, as I addressed him thus:
'Come, tell me, William, what these horrid noises are,
　　That do affright and so unsettle us.'

　　'Well, sir,' he said, 'Billy has murdered Ben,
And Kate has knifed her man and drowned her ailing child.'
' 'Twas ever thus,' I said, 'with maids and men.
　　Draw me another pint of old and mild.'

R. P. Lister (1914–　)

Tavern by the Sea

A distant glimmer
And a beacon spitting light
In the black face of night.

Everything is brine and yearning.

Winds with waves on their back
Make tremble the tavern
Which is an anchored ship.

Love passionate and brutal
Amidst the open knives
And the abandon
Of a prostitute's embrace.

Upon the air despairings rise
In heavy swells of smoke.

Bottles, glasses, bottles . . .
–Oh! the thirst of a sailor . . .

Tattooings pricked on skin
Proclaim the pain and the bravado
Of escapades in ports.

Men of every race,
Men without homeland or name
–Just men of the sea
With voice of salt and wind
And ships in unclouded eyes.

Boredom and longing appear
Chewing on aged pipes . . .
Appear and then depart
Staggering off with a drunk.

Cards, tables, and chairs,
Bottles, glasses, bottles
And the tavern-keeper's face
Stirring up ancient quarrels.

And everything is full of sin
And everything is full of sleep
And everything is full of sea!

Aquinaldo Fonseca (1922–   )

The Mermaid Tavern

Souls of Poets dead and gone,
What Elysium have ye known,
Happy field or mossy cavern,
Choicer than the Mermaid Tavern?
Have ye tippled drink more fine
Than mine host's Canary wine?

Or are fruits of Paradise
Sweeter than those dainty pies
Of venison? O generous food!
Drest as though bold Robin Hood
Would, with his Maid Marian,
Sup and bowse from horn and can.

I have heard that on a day
Mine host's signboard flew away
Nobody knew whither, till
An astrologer's old quill
To a sheepskin gave the story–
Said he saw you in your glory
Underneath a new-old Sign
Sipping beverage divine,
And pledging with contented smack
The Mermaid in the Zodiac.

Souls of Poets dead and gone,
What Elysium have ye known–
Happy field or mossy cavern–
Choicer than the Mermaid Tavern?

John Keats (1795–1821)

Tom Tatter's Birthday Ode

Come all you jolly dogs, in the Grapes, and King's Head, and
    Green Man, and Bell taps,
And shy up your hats–if you haven't hats, your paper and
    woollen caps,
Shout with me and cry Eureka! by the sweet Parnassian River
While echo, in Warner's Wood, replies, Huzza! the young
    Squire for ever!

And Vulcan, Mars, and Hector of Troy, and Jupiter and his
    wife,

And Phoebus, from his forked hill, coming down to take a
knife,
And Mercury, and piping Pan, to the tune of Old King Cole,
And Venus the Queen of Love, to eat an ox that was roasted
whole.

Sir Mark, God bless him, loves good old times, when beards
wag, and everything goes merry,
There'll be drinking out of gracecups, and a Boar's head
chewing rosemary,
Maid Marian, and a Morris dance, and the acting of quaint
Moralities,
Doctor Bellamy and a Hobby horse, and many other Old
Formalities.

But there won't be any Psalm-singing saints, to make us sad
of a Monday,
But Bacchus will preach to us out of a barrel, instead of the
methodist Bundy.
We'll drink to the King in good strong ale, like souls that are
true and loyal,
And a fig for Mrs Hanway, camomile, sage and pennyroyal;
And a fig for Master Gregory, that takes tipsy folk into
custody,
He was a wise man to-morrow, and will be a wiser man
yesterday.

Come fill a bumper up, my boys, and toss off every drop of
it!
Here's young Squire Ringwood's health, and may he live as
long as Jason,
Before Atropos cuts his thread, and Dick Tablet, the bungling
mason,
Chips him a marble tea-table, with a marble tea-urn a-top of
it!

Thomas Hood (1799–1845)

Class Incident from Graves

Wednesdays were guest night in the mess, when the colonel
expected the married officers, who usually dined at home, to
attend. The band played Gilbert and Sullivan music behind a
curtain. . . . Afterwards the bandmaster was invited to the
senior officer's table for his complimentary glass of Light or
Vintage.

(Good-bye to All That)

At the officers' table, for half an hour afterwards, port,
The bandmaster. He accepts, one drink long,
All the courtesy of the gentlemen. They are suave, and equal.
'I expect with your job . . . Do you find . . . Oh well. . . .'
The bandmaster edges the shining inch of port along the grain
    of the table,
Precisely covering one knot with the transparent
Base of the glass. He crouches forward over the polished
    wood
Towards the officers, not comfortably convivial,
Eyes always going to the face speaking next,
Deferential, very pleased.
The band put away their instruments out at the back, having
Drunk their beers, standing.
The detachable pieces of brass lie down
In the felt grooves of the cases, just as they should.
Nine-thirty strikes.
There is laughter of men together, coming from inside.
'Mitchell's still in there, hob-nobbing with the officers.'

Alan Brownjohn (1931–)

It is Later than You Think

Lone amid the café's cheer,
Sad of heart am I to-night;

51

Dolefully I drink my beer,
But no single line I write.
There's the wretched rent to pay,
Yet I glower at pen and ink:
Oh, inspire me, Muse, I pray,
It is later than you think!

Hello! there's a pregnant phrase.
Bravo! let me write it down;
Hold it with a hopeful gaze,
Gauge it with a fretful frown;
Tune it to my lyric lyre . . .
Ah! upon starvation's brink,
How the words are dark and dire:
It is later than you think.

Weigh them well. . . . Behold yon band,
Students drinking by the door,
Madly merry, *bock* in hand,
Saucers stacked to mark their score.
Get you gone, you jolly scamps;
Let your parting glasses clink;
Seek your long neglected lamps:
It is later than you think.

Look again: yon dainty blonde,
All allure and golden grace,
Oh so willing to respond
Should you turn a smiling face.
Play your part, poor pretty doll;
Feast and frolic, pose and prink;
There's the Morgue to end it all,
And it's later than you think.

Yon's a playwright—mark his face,
Puffed and purple, tense and tired;
Pasha-like he holds his place,
Hated, envied and admired.
How you gobble life, my friend;
Wine, and woman soft and pink!
Well, each tether has its end:
Sir, it's later than you think.

See yon living scarecrow pass
With a wild and wolfish stare
At each empty absinthe glass,
As if he saw Heaven there.
Poor damned wretch, to end your pain
There is still the Greater Drink.
Yonder waits the sanguine Seine . . .
It is later than you think.

Lastly, you who read: aye, you
Who this very line may scan:
Think of all you planned to do . . .
Have you done the best you can?
See! the tavern lights are low;
Black's the night, and how you shrink!
God! and is it time to go?
Ah! the clock is always slow;
It is later than you think;
Sadly later than you think;
Far, far later than you think.

Robert Service (1876–1958)

Yorkshiremen in Pub Gardens

As they sit there, happily drinking,
their strokes, cancers and so forth are not in their minds.
   Indeed, what earthly good would thinking
about the future (which is Death) do? Each summer finds
   beer in their hands in big pint glasses.
   And so their leisure passes.

   Perhaps the older ones allow some inkling
into their thoughts. Being hauled, as a kid, upstairs to bed

screaming for a teddy or a tinkling
musical box, against their will. Each Joe or Fred
    wants longer with the life and lasses.
    And so their time passes.

    Second childhood; and 'Come in, number 80!'
shouts inexorably the man in charge of the boating pool.
    When you're called you must go, matey,
so don't complain, keep it all calm and cool,
    there's masses of time yet, masses, masses . . .
    And so their life passes.

Gavin Ewart (1916–)

'The Saracen's Head'

'The Saracen's Head' looks down the lane,
Where we shall never drink wine again,
For the wicked old women who feel well-bred
Have turned to a tea-shop 'The Saracen's Head'.

'The Saracen's Head' out of Araby came,
King Richard riding in arms like flame,
And where he established his folks to be fed
He set up a spear—and the Saracen's Head.

But the 'Saracen's Head' outlived the Kings,
It thought and it thought of most horrible things,
Of Health and of Soap and of Standard Bread,
And of Saracen drinks at the 'Saracen's Head'.

So the 'Saracen's Head' fulfils its name,
They drink no wine—a ridiculous game—
And I shall wonder until I'm dead,
How it ever came into the Saracen's Head.

G. K. Chesterton (1874–1936)

ALEHOUSE YARNS

From Triads

Three things that are always ready in a decent man's house:
beer, a bath, a good fire.

Three scarcities that are better than abundance: a scarcity of
fancy talk, a scarcity of cows in a small pasture, a scarcity
of friends around the beer.

Versions: Thomas Kinsella (1928–   )

Paddy Murphy

The night that Paddy Murphy died
I never shall forget!
The whole damn town got stinking drunk
And they're not sober yet.

There is one thing they did that night
That filled me full of fear:
They took the ice right off the corpse
And stuck it in the beer.

That's how they showed their respect for Paddy Murphy,
That's how they showed their honour and their fight,

That's how they showed their respect for Paddy Murphy
They drank his health in ice-cold beer that night!

Anonymous

The Wild Rover

I've been a wild rover these seven long years,
I've spent all my money in ale and strong beers,
But the time has come my boys, to take better care,
Unless poverty happens to fall to my share.

Chorus
So therefore I'll lay up my money in store,
And I never will play the wild rover any more;
Wild rover, wild rover, wild rover, any more,
And then I will play the wild rover no more.

I went to an ale house where I used to resort,
I began for to tell them my money got short;
I asked them to trust me, but their answer was nay,
Such customers as you we may have every day.

Then my hands from my pockets I pulled out straightway,
Pulled a handful of gold out to hear what they'd say
O! here's ale, wine, and brandy, here's enough of the best,
It was only to try you, I was but in jest.

Begone you proud landlord, I bid you adieu,
For the devil of one penny will I spend with you;
For the money I've got boys, I'll take better care,
And I never will play the wild rover any more.

So now I'll go home to my sweet loving wife,
In hopes to live happy all the days of my life;

From rambling and roving, I'll take better care,
Unless poverty happens to fall to my share.

Anonymous

Kentucky Moonshiner

I've been a moonshiner for seventeen long years,
I've spent all my money for whiskey and beers.
I'll go to some holler, I'll pull up my still,
I'll make you a gallon for a two-dollar bill.

I'll go to some grocery and drink with my friends,
No woman to follow to see what I spends.
God bless those pretty women, I wish they were mine,
Their breath smells as sweet as the dew on the vine.

I'll eat when I'm hungry and drink when I'm dry,
If moonshine don't kill me, I'll live till I die.
God bless those moonshiners, I wish they were mine,
Their breath smells as sweet as the good old moonshine.

Anonymous

A Glass of Beer

The lanky hank of a she in the inn over there,
Nearly killed me for asking the loan of a glass of beer;
May the devil grip the whey-faced slut by the hair,
And beat bad manners out of her skin for a year.

That parboiled ape, with the toughest jaw you will see
On virtue's path, and a voice that would rasp the dead,
Came roaring and raging the minute she looked at me,
And threw me out of the house on the back of my head!

If I asked her master he'd give me a cask a day;
But she, with the beer at hand, not a gill would arrange!
May she marry a ghost and bear him a kitten, and may
The High King of Glory permit her to get the mange.

James Stephens (1882–1950)

What Tomas Said in a Pub

I saw God! Do you doubt it?
Do you dare to doubt it?
I saw the Almighty Man His hand
Was resting on a mountain! And
He looked upon the World, and all about it:
I saw Him plainer than you see me now
—You mustn't doubt it!

He was not satisfied?
His look was all dissatisfied!
His beard swung on a wind, far out of sight
Behind the world's curve! And there was light
Most fearful from His forehead! And He sighed—
—That star went always wrong, and from the start
I was dissatisfied!—

He lifted up His hand!
I say He heaved a dreadful hand
Over the spinning earth! Then I said,—Stay,
You must not strike it, God! I'm in the way!
And I will never move from where I stand!—

He said,—Dear child, I feared that you were dead,—
. . . And stayed His hand!

James Stephens (1882–1950)

never blame the booze

as i go up and down the town
hither to and fro i gather many a
smile and frown and talk of
thus and so i lately
listened and i heard two chaps
their luck bewail life did not get
a pleasant word they
told an awful tale for one of them
had just been fired he
glummed and wondered why he cried
into his beer
aspired
to punch the boss his eye too
true the other one exclaimed this
world s a burning shame the
game of living has been framed it is
a rotten game and ever as they railed
at fate and wooed the sombre muse
they steadily absorbed a great
sufficiency of booze but neither one
that cursed his luck and beat his burning bean
would blame the downfall on the truck
that passed his lips between
and as i listened there i thought it were
more candid far to give its dues to what they bought
across the varnished bar they should indeed
be far more frank about their hard lucks boss
they should remark
each genial tank unto their bosses faces

you can t expect a man to drink as much as i do boss
and have much time to work and think
and put the job across
oh boss you ask too much of me
i do the best i can but who can lush
continually and be a working man
you can t expect a man to booze from morning
until night and feel quite nimble
in his shoes and add his figures right oh boss
you ask too much of us we have no flair for toil
we d rather daily dally thus imbibing joyful oil
you can t expect a man to souse
and do work for your business house so do not be unjust
twere more like reason if they said such words
unto their bosses than tear the hair
and beat the head and blame luck
for their losses

                                                                archy

                              Don Marquis (1878–1937)

The Four Nights' Drunk

The first night when I come home, drunk as I could be,
I found this horse in the stable, where my horse ought to be.
    'Come here, little wifey! Explain yourself to me:
    Why is there a horse in the stable, where my horse ought
        to be?'
            'Why, you durn fool, you blame fool, can't you plainly
                see?
            It's only a milk cow my momma give to me.'
Now, I been living in this here world forty years and more.
And I never seen a milk cow with a saddle on before.

The second night when I come home, drunk as I could be,
I found a coat in the closet, where my coat ought to be.

'Come here, little wifey! Explain yourself to me:
Why is there a coat in the closet, where my coat ought to
     be?'
  'Why, you durn fool, you blame fool, can't you plainly
     see?
  It's only a coverlet my momma give to me.'
Now, I been living in this here world forty years and more,
And I never seen a coverlet with buttons on before.

The third night when I come home, drunk as I could be,
I found a hat hanging on the rack, where my hat ought to be.
  'Come here, little wifey! Explain yourself to me:
  Why is there a hat hanging on the rack, where my hat ought
     to be?'
     'Why, you durn fool, you blame fool, can't you plainly
        see?
     It's only a chamberpot my momma give to me.'
Now, I been living in this here world forty years and more,
And I never seen a J. B. Stetson chamberpot before.

The fourth night when I come home, drunk as I could be,
I found a head lying on the bed, where my head ought to
     be.
  'Come here, little wifey! Explain yourself to me:
  Why is there a head lying on the bed, where my head ought
     to be?'
     'Why, you durn fool, you blame fool, can't you plainly
        see?
     It's only a cabbage head my momma give to me.'
Now I been living in this here world forty years and more,
And I never seen a cabbage head with a mustache on before.

Anonymous

Advice to a Young Lady on the Subject of Alcohol

Beware the man who keeps you late
When Mum said to be in by ate,
And shun the chap who, at the Palais,
Invites you to inspect his chalais,
Behave, then, as you really ought,
Refuse that second glass of pought.
Supping unaccustomed liquor
Will only make you fall the quicor;
Drinking brandies at 'The Mitre'
Is sure to go and make you titre;
And oh! that headache in the dawn
Will make you wish you'd not been bawn.
Remember, then, a maiden oughter
Shun all drink, and stick to woughter.

Eric Parrott

Have You Seen the Lady?

'Have I told you the name of a lady?
Have I told you the name of a dear?
  'Twas known long ago,
  And ends with an O;
You don't hear it often round here.

Have I talked of the eyes of a lady?
Have I talked of the eyes that are bright?
  Their color, you see,
  Is B-L-U-E:
They're the gin in the cocktail of light.

Have I sung of the hair of a lady?
Have I sung of the hair of a dove?
  What shade do you say?
  B-L-A-C-K;
It's the fizz in the champagne of love.

Can you guess it—the name of the lady?
She is sweet, she is fair, she is coy.
  Your guessing forego,
It's J-U-N-O:
She's the mint in the julep of joy.'

> *John Philip Sousa* (1854–1932),
> (Composer of *The Stars and Stripes*
> *Forever* March)

Old Wife in High Spirits

In an Edinburgh Pub

An auld wumman cam' in, a mere rickle o' banes, in a faded
    black dress
And a bonnet wi' beads o jet rattlin' on it;
A puir-lookin' cratur, you'd think she could haurdly ha'e had
    less
Life left in her and still lived, but dagonit!

He gied her a stiff whisky—she was nervous as a troot
And could haurdly haud the tumbler, puir cratur;
Syne he gied her anither, joked wi' her, and anither, and syne
Wild as the whisky up cam' her nature.

The rod that struck water frae the rock in the desert
Was naething to the life that sprang oot o' her;
The dowie auld soul was twinklin' and fizzin' wi' fire;
You never saw ocht sae souple and kir.

Like a sackful o' monkeys she was, and her lauchin'
Loupit up whiles to incredible heights;
Wi' ane owre the eight her temper changed and her tongue
Flew juist as the forkt lichtnin' skites.

The heich skeich auld cat was fair in her element;
Wanton as a whirlwind, and shairly better that way
Than a'crippen thegither wi' laneliness and cauld
Like a foretaste o' the graveyaird clay.

Some folk nae doot'll condemn gie'in' a guid spree
To the puir dune body and raither she endit her days
Like some auld tashed copy o' the Bible yin sees
On a street book-barrow's tipenny trays.

A' I ken is weel-fed and weel-put-on though they be
Ninety per cent o' respectable folk never hae
As muckle life in their creeshy carcases frae beginnin' to end
As kythed in that wild auld carline that day!

Hugh MacDiarmid (1892–1978)

The Tankards

At the long tables of time
The Tankards of God carouse.
They empty the eyes of the seeing and the eyes of the blind,
The hearts of the ruling shadows,
The hollow cheek of evening.
They are the most mighty tipplers:
They drink up the full and they drink up the empty
And never foam over as you do and I.

Paul Celan (1920–   )

trans. by Ingo Seidler

Friar's Song

Some love the matin-chimes, which tell
   The hour of prayer to sinner;
But better far's the midday bell,
   Which speaks the hour of dinner;
For when I see a smoking fish,
   Or capon drowned in gravy,
Or noble haunch on silver dish,
   Full glad I sing my Ave.

My pulpit is an alehouse bench,
   Whereon I sit so jolly;
A smiling rosy country wench,
   My saint and patron holy.
I kiss her cheek so red and sleek,
   I press her ringlets wavy,
And in her willing ear I speak,
   A most religious Ave.

And if I'm blind, yet Heaven is kind,
   And holy saints forgiving;
For sure he leads a right good life,
   Who thus admires good living.
Above, they say, our flesh is air,
   Our blood celestial ichor:
Oh, grant! 'mid all the changes there,
   They may not change our liquor!

      William Makepeace Thackeray
          (1811–1863)

Nunc Viridant Segetes

The standing corn is green, the wild in flower,
   The vines are swelling, 'tis the sweet o' the year,

Bright-winged the birds, and heavens shrill with song,
　　And laughing sea and earth and every star.

But with it all, there's never a drink for me,
　　No wine, nor mead, nor even a drop of beer.
Ah, how hath failed that substance manifold,
　　Born of the kind earth and the dewy air!

I am a writer, I, a musician, Orpheus the second,
　　And the ox that treads out the corn, and your well-wisher
　　　I,
I am your champion armed with the weapons of wisdom and
　　logic,
　　Muse, tell my lord bishop and father his servant is dry.

Sedulius Scottus (Ninth Century)

Athabaska Dick

When the boys come out from Lac Labiche in the lure of the
　　early Spring.
To take the pay of the 'Hudson's Bay', as their fathers did
　　before,
They are all a-glee for the jamboree, and they make the
　　Landing ring
With a whoop and a whirl, and a 'Grab your girl', and a rip
　　and a skip and a roar.
For the spree of Spring is a sacred thing, and the boys must
　　have their fun;
Packer and tracker and half-breed Cree, from the boat to the
　　bar they leap;
And then when the long flotilla goes, and the last of their pay
　　is done,
The boys from the banks of Lac Labiche swing to the heavy
　　sweep.

66

And oh, how they sigh! and their throats are dry, and sorry
are they and sick:
Yet there's none so cursed with a lime-kiln thirst as that
Athabaska Dick.

He was long and slim and lean of limb, but strong as a stripling
bear;
And by the right of his skill and might he guided the Long
Brigade.
All water-wise were his laughing eyes, and he steered with a
careless care,
And he shunned the shock of foam and rock, till they came
to the Big Cascade.
And here they must make the long *portage*, and the boys
sweat in the sun;
And they heft and pack, and they haul and track, and each
must do his trick;
But their thoughts are far in the Landing bar, where the founts
of nectar run:
And no man thinks of such gorgeous drinks as that Athabaska
Dick.

'Twas the close of day and his long boat lay just over the Big
Cascade,
When there came to him one Jack-pot Jim, with a wild light
in his eye;
And he softly laughed, and he led Dick aft, all eager, yet half
afraid,
And snugly stowed in his coat he showed a pilfered flask of
'rye'.
And in haste he slipped, or in fear he tripped, but—Dick in
warning roared—
And there rang a yell, and it befell that Jim was overboard.

Oh, I heard a splash, and quick as a flash I knew he could
not swim.
I saw him whirl in the river swirl, and thresh his arms about.
In a queer, strained way I heard Dick say: 'I'm going after
him,'
Throw off his coat, leap down the boat—and then I gave a
shout:

'Boys, grab him, quick! You're crazy, Dick! Far better one
  than two!
'Hell, man! You know you've got no show! It's sure and
  certain death . . .'
And there we hung, and there we clung, with beef and brawn
  and thew,
And sinews cracked and joints were racked, and panting came
  our breath;
And there we swayed and there we prayed, till strength and
  hope were spent—
Then Dick, he threw us off like rats, and after Jim he went.

With mighty urge amid the surge of river-rage he leapt,
And gripped his mate and desperate he fought to gain the
  shore;
With teeth a-gleam he bucked the stream, yet swift and sure
  he swept
To meet the mighty cataract that waited all a-roar.
And there we stood like carven wood, our faces sickly white,
And watched him as he beat the foam, and inch by inch he
  lost;
And nearer, nearer drew the fall, and fiercer grew the fight,
Till on the very cascade crest a last farewell he tossed.
Then down and down and down they plunged into that pit of
  dread;
And mad we tore along the shore to claim our bitter dead.

And from that hell of frenzied foam, that crashed and fumed
  and boiled,
Two little bodies bubbled up, and they were heedless then;
And oh, they lay like senseless clay! and bitter hard we toiled,
Yet never, never gleam of hope, and we were weary men.
And moments mounted into hours, and black was our despair;
And faint were we, and we were fain to give them up as dead,
When suddenly I thrilled with hope: 'Back, boys! and give
  him air;
'I feel the flutter of his heart. . . .' And, as the word I said,
Dick gave a sigh and gazed around, and saw our breathless
  band;
And saw the sky's blue floor above, all strewn with golden
  fleece;

And saw his comrade Jack-pot Jim, and touched him with his
 hand:
And then there came into his eyes a look of perfect peace.
And as there, at his very feet, the thwarted river raved,
I heard him murmur low and deep:
        'Thank God! the *whiskey's* saved.'

Robert Service (1876–1958)

In a Prominent Bar in Secaucus One Day

In a prominent bar in Secaucus one day
Rose a lady in skunk with a topheavy sway,
Raised a knobby red finger—all turned from their beer—
While with eyes bright as snowcrust she sang high and clear:

'Now who of you'd think from an eyeload of me
That I once was a lady as proud as could be?
Oh I'd never sit down by a tumbledown drunk
If it wasn't, my dears, for the high cost of junk.

'All the gents used to swear that the white of my calf
Beat the down of the swan by a length and a half.
In the kerchief of linen I caught to my nose
Ah, there never fell snot, but a little gold rose.

'I had seven gold teeth and a toothpick of gold,
My Virginia cheroot was a leaf of it rolled
And I'd light it each time with a thousand in cash—
Why the bums used to fight if I flicked them an ash.

'Once the toast of the Biltmore, the belle of the Taft,
I would drink bottle beer at the Drake, never draft,
And dine at the Astor on Salisbury steak
With a clean tablecloth for each bite I did take.

'In a car like the Roxy I'd roll to the track,
A steel-guitar trio, a bar in the back,
And the wheels made no noise, they turned over so fast,
Still it took you ten minutes to see me go past.

'When the horses bowed down to me that I might choose,
I bet on them all, for I hated to lose.
Now I'm saddled each night for my butter and eggs
And the broken threads race down the backs of my legs.

'Let you hold in mind, girls, that your beauty must pass
Like a lovely white clover that rusts with its grass.
Keep your bottoms off barstools and marry you young
Or be left—an old barrel with many a bung.

'For when time takes you out for a spin in his car
You'll be hard-pressed to stop him from going too far
And be left by the roadside, for all your good deeds,
Two toadstools for tits and a face full of weeds.'

All the house raised a cheer, but the man at the bar
Made a phonecall and up pulled a red patrol car
And she blew us a kiss as they copped her away
From that prominent bar in Secaucus, N.J.

X. J. Kennedy (1929–   )

I taste a liquor never brewed

I taste a liquor never brewed,
From tankards scooped in pearl;
Not all the vats upon the Rhine
Yield such an alcohol!

Inebriate of air am I,
And debauchee of dew,

Reeling, through endless summer days,
From inns of molten blue.

When landlords turn the drunken bee
Out of the foxglove's door,
When butterflies renounce their drams,
I shall but drink the more!

Till seraphs swing their snowy hats,
And saints to windows run,
To see the little tippler
Leaping against the sun!

Emily Dickinson (1830–1886)

Point of No Return

When the alcoholic passed the crucial point
Of no return, he sold his soul to priests
Who, mercifully, would not deny him drink
But remitted a thousand years of purgatory
On this condition: that he must now engage
A woman's pity, beseeching her to cure him,
Wearing her down with betterment and relapse,
Till he has won a second soul for glory,
At the point of no return.

Robert Graves (1895–1986)

Cast Away Care

Cast away care; he that loves sorrow
   Lengthens not a day, nor can buy to-morrow;

Money is trash; and he that will spend it,
Let him drink merrily, Fortune will send it.
    Merrily, merrily, merrily, oh, ho!
    Play it off stiffly, we may not part so.

Wine is a charm, it heats the blood too,
Cowards it will harm, if the wine be good too;
Quickens the wit, and makes the back able;
Scorn to submit to the watch or constable.
    Merrily, merrily, etc.

Pots fly about, give us more liquor,
Brothers of a rout, our brains will flow quicker;
Empty the cask; score it up we care not,
Fill up the pots again, and drink on and spare not.
    Merrily, merrily, etc.

Thomas Dekker (1510–1632)

Porter's speech

Porter. . . . drink, sir, is a great provoker of three things.
Macduff. What three things does drink especially provoke?
Porter. Marry, sir, nose-painting, sleep, and urine. Lechery,
sir, it provokes, and unprovokes: it provokes the desire, but it
takes away the performance. Therefore much drink may be
said to be an equivocator with lechery: it makes him, and it
mars him; it sets him on, and it takes him off; it persuades him,
and disheartens him; makes him stand to, and not stand to; in
conclusion, equivocates him in a sleep, and, giving him the lie,
leaves him.

William Shakespeare, Macbeth (1564–1616)

Survey of Literature

In all the good Greek of Plato
I lack my roastbeef and potato.

A better man was Aristotle,
Pulling steady on the bottle.

I dip my hat to Chaucer,
Swilling soup from his saucer.

And to Master Shakespeare
Who wrote big on small beer.

The abstemious Wordsworth
Subsisted on a curd's-worth,

But a slick one was Tennyson,
Putting gravy on his venison.

What these men had to eat and drink
Is what we say and what we think.

The influence of Milton
Came wry out of Stilton.

Sing a song for Percy Shelley,
Drowned in pale lemon jelly.

And for precious John Keats,
Dripping blood of pickled beets.

Then there was poor Willie Blake,
He foundered on sweet cake.

God have mercy on the sinner
Who must write with no dinner,

No gravy and no grub,
No pewter and no pub,

No belly and no bowels,
Only consonants and vowels.

John Crowe Ransom (1888–1974)

The Thirsty Poet

So pass my Days. But when Nocturnal Shades
This World invelop, and th' inclement Air
Persuades Men to repel benumming Frosts
With pleasant Wines, and crackling Blaze of Wood;
Me lonely sitting, nor the glimmering Light
Of Make-weight Candle, nor the joyous Talk
Of loving Friend delights; distress'd, forlorn,
Amidst the Horrors of the tedious Night,
Darkling I sigh, and feed with dismal Thoughts
My anxious Mind; or sometimes mournful Verse
Indite, and sing of Groves and Myrtle Shades,
Or desperate Lady near a purling Stream,
Or Lover pendent on a Willow-Tree:
Mean while, I labour with eternal Drought,
And restless wish, and rave; my parched Throat
Finds no Relief, nor heavy Eyes Repose:
But if a Slumber haply does invade
My weary Limbs, my Fancy, still awake,
Thoughtful of Drink, and eager, in a Dream
Tipples imaginary Pots of Ale:
In vain; awake I find the settled Thirst
Still gnawing, and the pleasant Phantom curse.
  Thus do I live from Pleasure quite debarr'd,
Nor taste the Fruits that the Sun's genial Rays
Mature, *John-Apple*, nor the downy *Peach*,

Nor *Walnut* in rough-farrow'd Coat secure,
Nor *Medlar*, Fruit delicious in Decay.

John Philips (1676–1709)

Interview with Doctor Drink

I have a fifth of therapy
In the house, and transference there.
Doctor, there's not much wrong with me,
Only a sick rattlesnake somewhere

In the house, if it be there at all,
But the lithe mouth is coiled. The shapes
Of door and window move. I call.
What is it that pulls down the drapes,

Disheveled and exposed? Your rye
Twists in my throat: intimacy
Is like hard liquor. Who but I
Coil there and squat, and pay your fee?

J. V. Cunningham (1911–   )

The Absinthe Drinker

For years I tried to leave them,
leave them all.
Now they've left me.
Three childish smiles are scars
inside my mind.
            She took all three.

My head breaks. The hours
slash my skull to splintered bone.

I wish there was a picture
I could hang to break the sight
of the wall across this room
with its hook of stone.

Where is my Dégas lady?
I carried her for years inside my poems
and hung her on the wall to comfort me.
Somewhere in a box of broken books
she sits, sipping her absinthe.
Now for the first time
I would drink with her.

Patrick Lane (1939–)

The Arrest of Oscar Wilde at the Cadogan Hotel

He sipped at a weak hock and seltzer
    As he gazed at the London skies
Through the Nottingham lace of the curtains
    Or was it his bees-winged eyes?

To the right and before him Pont Street
    Did tower in her new built red,
As hard as the morning gaslight
    That shone on his unmade bed,

'I want some more hock in my seltzer,
    And Robbie, please give me your hand—
Is this the end or beginning?
    How can I understand?

'So you've brought me the latest *Yellow Book:*
    And Buchan has got in it now:
Approval of what is approved of
    Is as false as a well-kept vow.

'More hock, Robbie—where is the seltzer?
    Dear boy, pull again at the bell!
They are all little better than *cretins*,
    Though this *is* the Cadogan Hotel.

'One astrakhan coat is at Willis's—
    Another one's at the Savoy:
Do fetch my morocco portmanteau,
    And bring them on later, dear boy.'

A thump, and a murmur of voices—
    ('Oh why must they make such a din?')
As the door of the bedroom swung open
    And TWO PLAIN CLOTHES POLICEMEN came in:

'Mr Woilde, we 'ave come for tew take yew
    Where felons and criminals dwell:
We must ask yew tew leave with us quoietly
    For this *is* the Cadogan Hotel.'

He rose, and he put down *The Yellow Book*.
    He staggered—and, terrible-eyed,
He brushed past the palms on the staircase
    And was helped to a hansom outside.

                    John Betjeman (1906–1985)

25 December 1960
(For Dylan Thomas)

Ward 130 in the passage on the right.
It's five in the morning and the milk-cart

has gone by with its horses, their eyes gleaming
in the bayonet-points of the street lights.
25 December 1960.
The children sleep
in Christmas stockings between satellites
hobby-horses, revolvers and toffees.
Sleep before the sirens of the sun
before the bombers of the butterflies.
Sleep in your Christmas stockings and candles.
On Hospital Hill stands a blazing tree.
Ward 130 in the passage on the right.
'Sure he drank a bottle of brandy
and lay for hours in an oxygen tent.
You know he was an alcoholic from
his first glass.' (Look, the day's
bright gun-barrel takes aim over the city!)
'Ah yes but, he himself once said
he had a harking after his dead God.
His final words? No
he lay quiet and with eyes wide open.'
Ward 130. He's been attended to
the eyes closed the hands already folded,
the whole room like a shield uplifted.

And on the windowsill and against the light
the praying mantis in unending prayer.

Ingrid Jonker (1933–1965)

Blaming Sons
An Apology for his own Drunkenness, AD 406

White hairs cover my temples,
I am wrinkled and gnarled beyond repair,
And though I have got five sons,
They all hate paper and brush.

A-shu is eighteen:
For laziness there is none like him.
A-hsüan does his best,
But really loathes the Fine Arts.
Yung and Tuan are thirteen,
But do not know 'six' from 'seven'.
T'ung-tzu in his ninth year
Is only concerned with things to eat.
If Heaven treats me like this,
What can I do but fill my cup?

T'ao Ch'ien (365–427)
trans. Arthur Waley

Drinking Dirge

A thousand years ago I used to dine
  In houses where they gave me such regale
Of dear companionship and comrades fine
  That out I went alone beyond the pale;
And riding, laughed and dared the skies malign
  To show me all the undiscovered tale–
But my philosophy's no more divine,
  I put my pleasure in a pint of ale.

And you, my friends, oh! pleasant friends of mine,
  Who leave me now alone, without avail,
On Californian hills you gave me wine,
  You gave me cider-drink in Longuevaille;
If after many years you come to pine
  For comradeship that is an ancient tale–
You'll find me drinking beer in Dead Man's Chine.
  I put my pleasure in a pint of ale.

In many a briny boat I've tried the brine,
  From many a hidden harbour I've set sail,

Steering towards the sunset where there shine
  The distant amethystine islands pale.
There are no ports beyond the far sea-line,
  Nor any halloa to meet the mariner's hail;
I stand at home and slip the anchor-line.
  I put my pleasure in a pint of ale.

Envoi

Prince! Is it true that when you go to dine
  You bring your bottle in a freezing pail?
Why then you cannot be a friend of mine.
  I put my pleasure in a pint of ale.

Hilaire Belloc (1870–1953)

The Old Familiar Faces

I have had playmates, I have had companions
In my days of childhood, in my joyful school-days;
  All, all are gone, the old familiar faces.

I have been laughing, I have been carousing,
Drinking late, sitting late, with my bosom cronies;
  All, all are gone, the old familiar faces.

I loved a love once, fairest among women:
Closed are her doors on me, I must not see her–
  All, all are gone, the old familiar faces.

I have a friend, a kinder friend has no man:
Like an ingrate, I left my friend abruptly;
  Left him, to muse on the old familiar faces.

Ghost-like I paced round the haunts of my childhood,
Earth seem'd a desert I was bound to traverse,
  Seeking to find the old familiar faces.

Friend of my bosom, thou more than a brother,
Why wert not thou born in my father's dwelling?
  So might we talk of the old familiar faces.

How some they have died, and some they have left me,
And some are taken from me; all are departed;
  All, all are gone, the old familiar faces.

Charles Lamb (1775–1834)

Last Will of the Drunk

Lay me in the woodbox,
Pack me with kindling,
Feed me a doctor with pills in his hair.
My eyes are his olives; prick them with toothpicks.
Give me a drink;
Take down the emptiness,
And pour in the colour.
Blow the man down, with the popping of corks.
Lift up the window-pane, with the nail of your finger;
Give me the eating of the outside air.
Turn up your overcoat at open umbrellas;
Mine is the collar that needs no forgiveness.
I charge thee with murder, thou foul-smelling rat.
While you're awaking, whine for forgiveness.
Mine is the horse that wins on the racetrack,
Mine is the jukebox that takes in the loot.
Smile, with your hair turning grey as you bellylaugh.
I am the power, and I have forgiveness.
But you have a pony, a small little thing;
Break up its milknest, and pour out its wings.
The earth is empty, and the sky is blued over;
Paint out my eyes, and ink out the sentinels.

I am a packleader;
Give me a drink.

Myra Von Riedemann (1935–   )

This is what

This is what I now propose:
In a tavern I shall die
With a glass up to my nose
And God's angels standing by
That they may indeed declare
As I take my final tot
May God receive with loving care
Such a decent drunken sot.

Fourteenth-century Latin toast

DRUNKENNESS

Anacreontic

Born I was to be old,
    And for to die here:
After that, in the mould
    long for to lie here.
But before that day comes,
    Still I be bousing;
For I know, in the tombs
    There's no carousing.

> Robert Herrick
> (1591–1674)

Inscribed on a Pint-Pot

There are several reasons for drinking,
And one has just entered my head;
If a man cannot drink when he's living
How the Hell can he drink when he's dead?

> Anonymous

The Irish Pig

'Twas an evening in November,
As I very well remember,
I was strolling down the street in drunken pride,
But my knees were all aflutter,
So I landed in the gutter,
And a pig came up and lay down by my side.

Yes, I lay there in the gutter
Thinking thoughts I could not utter,
When a colleen passing by did softly say,
'Ye can tell a man that boozes
By the company he chooses.'
At that the pig got up and walked away!

Anonymous

Love

There's the wonderful love of a beautiful maid,
    And the love of a staunch true man,
And the love of a baby that's unafraid–
    All have existed since time began.
But the most wonderful love, the Love of all loves,
    Even greater than the love for Mother,
Is the infinite, tenderest, passionate love
    Of one dead drunk for another.

Anonymous

The horse and mule

The horse and mule live 30 years
And nothing know of wines and beers.
The goat and sheep at 20 die
And never taste of Scotch or Rye.
The cow drinks water by the ton
And at 18 is mostly done.
The dog at 15 cashes in
Without the aid of rum and gin.
The cat in milk and water soaks
And then in 12 short years it croaks.
The modest, sober, bone-dry hen
Lay eggs for nogs, then dies at 10.
All animals are strictly dry;
They sinless live and swiftly die;
But sinful, ginful, rum-soaked men
Survive for three score years and ten.
And some of them, a very few,
Stay pickled till they're 92.

Anonymous

Forever Ambrosia

Calypso
Is a bit of a dipso,
She can't keep up her pants, they slip so.

She always telegraphs her punches
By serving those ambrosial lunches.

And after getting Ulysses blotto
Leads him to her private grotto.

The Ancient Mariner tires of nectar
Had without benefit of rector,

And hankering to hoist Blue Peter
Gets so he's afraid to meet her.

After seven years, one afternoon
She says: 'You're not *going*? What, so soon?'

Sadly the hero reaffirms:
'I can't be immortal on your terms.

'No can do. Even in a cave
I'm too pooped to misbehave.

'Listen, lady, it simply shows ya
Men can't live just on ambrosia.'

Calypso laughed and laughed and laughed.
'Okay; I'll help you build a raft.'

Christopher Morley (1890–1957)

On Bibinus, a notorious drunkard

The sot Loserus is drunk twice a day,
Bibinus only once; now of these say
Which may a man the greatest drunkard call?
Bibinus still; for he's drunk once for all.

Sir Edward Sherburne (1618–1702)

Stag Night, Palaeolithic

Drink deep to Uncle Uglug,
That early heroic human,
The first to eat an oyster,
The first to marry a woman.

God's curse on him who murmurs
As the banquet waxes moister,
'Had he only eaten the woman,
Had he only married the oyster!'

Ogden Nash (1902–1971)

The Logical Vegetarian

You will find me drinking rum,
    Like a sailor in a slum,
You will find me drinking beer like a Bavarian,
    You will find me drinking gin
    In the lowest kind of inn,
Because I am a rigid Vegetarian.

    So I cleared the inn of wine,
    And I tried to climb the sign,
And I tried to hail the constable as 'Marion'.
    But he said I couldn't speak
    And he bowled me to the Beak
Because I was a happy Vegetarian.

    Oh, I knew a Doctor Gluck,
    And his nose it had a hook,
And his attitudes were anything but Aryan;
    So I gave him all the pork
    That I had, upon a fork;
Because I am myself a Vegetarian.

I am silent in the club,
I am silent in the pub,
I am silent on a bally peak in Darien;
   For I stuff away for life
   Shoving peas in with a knife,
Because I am at heart a Vegetarian.

   No more the milk of cows
   Shall pollute my private house
Than the milk of the wild mares of the Barbarian;
   I will stick to port and sherry,
   For they are so very, very,
So very, very, very Vegetarian.

G. K. Chesterton (1874–1936)

The Rolling English Road

Before the Roman came to Rye or out to Severn strode,
The rolling English drunkard made the rolling English road.
A reeling road, a rolling road, that rambles round the shire,
And after him the parson ran, the sexton and the squire;
A merry road, a mazy road, and such as we did tread
That night we went to Birmingham by way of Beachy Head.

I knew no harm of Bonaparte and plenty of the Squire,
And for to fight the Frenchmen I did not much desire;
But I did bash their baggonets because they came arrayed
To straighten out the crooked road an English drunkard
    made,
Where you and I went down the lane with ale-mugs in our
    hands,
The night we went to Glastonbury by way of Goodwin Sands.

His sins they were forgiven him; or why do flowers run
Behind him; and the hedges all strengthening in the sun?
The wild thing went from left to right and knew not which
    was which,
But the wild rose was above him when they found him in the
    ditch.
God pardon us, nor harden us; we did not see so clear
The night we went to Bannockburn by way of Brighton Pier.

My friends, we will not go again or ape an ancient rage,
Or stretch the folly of our youth to be the shame of age,
But walk with clearer eyes and ears this path that wandereth,
And see undrugged in evening light the decent inn of death;
For there is good news yet to hear and fine things to be seen,
Before we go to Paradise by way of Kensal Green.

G. K. Chesterton (1874–1936)

The Rake's Progress

Born lorn,
Dad bad,
Nurse worse;
'Drat brat!'
School – Fool,
Work – shirk
Gal pal,
Splash cash,
Bets – debts,
Pop shop.
Nil – Till!
Boss – loss
Wired 'Fired!'
Scrub pub,
Drink – Brink –
Found Drowned.

'De se';
Grief brief.

C. W. Brodribb (1878–1945)

Epigram on an academic Visit to the Continent

I went to Frankfort, and got drunk
With that most learn'd professor—Brunck:
I went to Worts, and got more drunken
With that more learn'd professor—Ruhncken.

Richard Porson (1759–1808)

Tarpauling Jacket

I am a young jolly brisk sailor,
   Delights in all manner of sport,
When I'm in liquor I'm mellow,
   The girls I then merrily court.
But love is surrounded with trouble,
   And puts such strange thoughts in my head,
Is it not a terrible story,
   That love it should strike me stone dead?

Here's a health to my friends and acquaintance,
   When death for me it doth come,
And let them behave in their station
   And send me a cask of good rum,
Let it be good royal stingo,

With three barrels of beer,
To make my friends the more welcome
    When they meet me at derry down fair.

Let there be six sailors to carry me,
    Let them be damnable drunk,
And as they are going to bury me,
    Let them fall down with my trunk.
Let there be no sighing and sobbing,
    But one single favour I crave,
Take me up in a tarpauling jacket,
    And fiddle and dance to my grave.

Anonymous

The Drunken Fisherman

Wallowing in this bloody sty,
I cast for fish that pleased my eye
(Truly Jehovah's bow suspends
No pots of gold to weight its ends);
Only the blood-mouthed rainbow trout
Rose to my bait. They flopped about
My canvas creel until the moth
Corrupted its unstable cloth.

A calendar to tell the day;
A handkerchief to wave away
The gnats; a couch unstuffed with storm
Pouching a bottle in one arm;
A whiskey bottle full of worms;
And bedroom slacks: are these fit terms
To mete the worm whose molten rage
Boils in the belly of old age?

Once fishing was a rabbit's foot–
O wind blow cold, O wind blow hot,
Let suns stay in or suns step out:
Life danced a jig on the sperm-whale's spout–
The fisher's fluent and obscene
Catches kept his conscience clean.
Children, the raging memory drools
Over the glory of past pools.

Now the hot river, ebbing, hauls
Its bloody waters into holes;
A grain of sand inside my shoe
Mimics the moon that might undo
Man and Creation too; remorse,
Stinking, has puddled up its source;
Here tantrums thrash to a whale's rage.
This is the pot-hole of old age.

Is there no way to cast my hook
Out of this dynamited brook?
The Fisher's sons must cast about
When shallow waters peter out.
I will catch Christ with a greased worm,
And when the Prince of Darkness stalks
My bloodstream to its Stygian term . . .
On water the Man-Fisher walks.

Robert Lowell (1917–1977)

Mr Flood's Party

Old Eben Flood, climbing alone one night
Over the hill between the town below
And the forsaken upland hermitage
That held as much as he should ever know
On earth again of home, paused warily.

The road was his with not a native near;
And Eben, having leisure, said aloud,
For no man else in Tilbury Town to hear:

'Well, Mr Flood, we have the harvest moon
Again, and we may not have many more;
The bird is on the wing, the poet says,
And you and I have said it here before.
Drink to the bird.' He raised up to the light
The jug that he had gone so far to fill,
And answered huskily: 'Well, Mr Flood,
Since you propose it, I believe I will.'

Alone, as if enduring to the end
A valiant armor of scarred hopes outworn,
He stood there in the middle of the road
Like Roland's ghost winding a silent horn.
Below him, in the town among the trees,
Where friends of other days had honored him,
A phantom salutation of the dead
Rang thinly till old Eben's eyes were dim.

Then, as a mother lays her sleeping child
Down tenderly, fearing it may awake,
He set the jug down slowly at his feet
With trembling care, knowing that most things break;
And only when assured that on firm earth
It stood, as the uncertain lives of men
Assuredly did not, he paced away,
And with his hand extended paused again:

'Well, Mr Flood, we have not met like this
In a long time; and many a change has come
To both of us, I fear, since last it was
We had a drop together. Welcome home!'
Convivially returning with himself,
Again he raised the jug up to the light;
And with an acquiescent quaver said:
'Well, Mr Flood, if you insist, I might.

'Only a very little, Mr Flood–
'For auld lang syne. No more, sir; that will do.'
So, for the time, apparently it did,
And Eben evidently thought so too;
For soon amid the silver loneliness
Of night he lifted up his voice and sang,
Secure, with only two moons listening,
Until the whole harmonious landscape rang–

'For auld lang syne.' The weary throat gave out,
The last word wavered, and the song was done.
He raised again the jug regretfully
And shook his head, and was again alone.
There was not much that was ahead of him,
And there was nothing in the town below–
Where strangers would have shut the many doors
That many friends had opened long ago.

Edwin Arlington Robinson (1869–1935)

Fable of the mermaid and the drunks

All these gentlemen were there inside
when she entered, utterly naked.
They had been drinking, and began to spit at her.
Recently come from the river, she understood nothing.
She was a mermaid who had lost her way.
The taunts flowed over her glistening flesh.
Obscenities drenched her golden breasts.
A stranger to tears, she did not weep.
A stranger to clothes, she did not dress.
They pocked her with cigarette ends and with burnt corks,
and rolled on the tavern floor with laughter.
She did not speak, since speech was unknown to her.
Her eyes were the colour of faraway love,
her arms were matching topazes.

Her lips moved soundlessly in coral light,
and ultimately, she left by that door.
Scarcely had she entered the river than she was cleansed,
gleaming once more like a white stone in the rain:
and without a backward look, she swam once more,
swam towards nothingness, swam to her dying.

Pablo Neruda (1904–1973)

Inscribed on the Arbor of the Old Drunkard (Tsui-weng't'ing) at Ch'u-chou

At forty, a man's not yet old,
'Old Drunkard' is just the way I sign my name.
A drunkard takes his leave of all things,
How could I then recall my age?

I love only the water below the arbor,
It comes somewhere from those jagged peaks.
It sounds as if falling from the sky,
Cascading down the eaves when it rains.
As it flows into the brook beneath the cliff,
Each drop adds to the hidden spring.
Its echoes never jar the ear like the voices of men,
Though its music is not that of pipes and strings.
Not that I don't find pleasure in strings and pipes,
But their notes at times are shrill and loud.

That's why I often bring my wine when I come,
And take long walks to get close to the waterfall.
Birds in the wilds peer at me as I lie drunk,
Clouds above the brook induce me to stay and take my rest.
Mountain flowers have no expression but a smile.
They do not know how to talk with me.

There's only the wind from the cliffs,
That blows upon me until I'm sober again.

Ou-yang Hsiu (1007–1072)
trans. Irving Y. Lo

The Corrupt Man in the French Pub

'I'm corrupt' he said to me in the French,
'I think I live in corruption's stench.'
Did this mean something about pay
Or those he was about to betray?
Was he selling out for a screw with a wrench
Or selling his wife six times a day?
'I'm corrupt' is a big thing to say
Though your chair is not a park bench.
I know that I am called corrupt myself
When seen around in good health
(By journalists usually)
And also because I get away
With 'not working' and such
Soi-disant words in inverted commas.
So in the common eye my form is
Perverted. An accusation to be ignored
Only the mind can be corrupt with a word.
So I asked him what he meant by corruption.
He said he was drinking too much.

Brian Higgins (1930–1965)

Anacreontic to Flip

Stingo! to thy bar-room skip,
Make a foaming mug of Flip;
Make it our country's staple,
Rum New England, Sugar Maple,
Beer, that's brewed from hops and Pumpkin,
Grateful to the thirsty Bumkin.
Hark! I hear thy poker fizzle,
And o'er the mug the liquor drizzle;
All against the earthen mug,
I hear the horn-spoon's cheerful dub;
I see thee, STINGO, take the Flip,
And sling thy cud from under lip,
Then pour more rum, and, bottle stopping,
Stir it again, and swear 'tis topping.
   Come quickly bring the humming liquor,
Richer than ale of British vicar;
Better than usquebaugh Hibernian,
Or than Flaccus' famed Falernian;
More potent, healthy, racy, frisky,
Than Holland's gin, or Georgia whisky.
Come, make a ring around the fire,
And hand the mug unto the Squire;
Here, Deacon, take the elbow chair,
And Ensign, Holiday, sit there:
You take the dye-tub, you the churn,
And I'll the double corner turn.
   See the mantling liquor rise!
And burn their cheeks, and close their eyes,
See the sideling mug incline—
Hear them curse their dull divine,
Who, on Sunday, dared to rail,
At *Brewster*'s flip, or *Downer*'s ale.
—Quick, Stingo, fly and bring another,
The Deacon here shall pay for t'other,
Ensign and I the third will share,
It's due on swop, for pie-bald mare.

Royall Tyler (1757–1826)

The Fly
An Anacreontick

Busy, curious, thirsty Fly,
Gently drink, and drink as I;
Freely welcome to my Cup,
Could'st thou sip, and sip it up;
Make the most of Life you may,
Life is short and wears away.

Just alike, both mine and thine,
Hasten quick to their Decline;
Thine's a Summer, mine's no more,
Though repeated to threescore;
Threescore Summers when they're gone,
Will appear as short as one.

William Oldys (1687–1761)

On John Dove, Innkeeper, Mauchline

Here lies Johnnie Pigeon;
What was his religion,
   Whe'er desires to ken,
To some ither warl'
Maun follow the carl,
   For here Johnnie Pigeon had nanc.

Strong ale was ablution,
Small beer persecution,
   A dram was *memento mori*;
But a full flowing bowl
Was the saving his soul,
   And port was celestial glory.

Robert Burns (1759–1796)

A Cider Song

To J. S. M.

Extract from a Romance which is not yet written and probably
never will be.

The wine they drink in Paradise
They make in Haute Lorraine;
God brought it burning from the sod
To be a sign and signal rod
That they that drink the blood of God
Shall never thirst again.

The wine they praise in Paradise
They make in Ponterey,
The purple wine of Paradise,
But we have better at the price;
It's wine they praise in Paradise,
It's cider that they pray.

The wine they want in Paradise
They find in Plodder's End,
The apple wine of Hereford,
Of Hafod Hill and Hereford,
Where woods went down to Hereford,
And there I had a friend.

The soft feet of the blessed go
In the soft western vales,
The road the silent saints accord,
The road from heaven to Hereford,
Where the apple wood of Hereford
Goes all the way to Wales.

G. K. Chesterton (1874–1936)

A Drunken Man's Praise of Sobriety

Come swish around, my pretty punk,
And keep me dancing still
That I may stay a sober man
Although I drink my fill.
Sobriety is a jewel
That I do much adore;
And therefore keep me dancing
Though drunkards lie and snore.
O mind your feet, O mind your feet,
Keep dancing like a wave,
And under every dancer
A dead man in his grave.
No ups and downs, my pretty,
A mermaid, not a punk;
A drunkard is a dead man,
And all dead men are drunk.

William Butler Yeats (1865–1936)

R–E–M–O–R–S–E

The cocktail is a pleasant drink;
It's mild and harmless—I don't think.
When you've had one, you call for two,
And then you don't care what you do.
Last night I hoisted twenty-three
Of those arrangements into me.
My wealth increased, I swelled with pride,
I was pickled, primed and ossified;
But R–E–M–O–R–S–E!
The water wagon is the place for me.
I think that somewhere in the game
I wept and told my real name.

At four I sought my whirling bed;
At eight I woke with such a head!
It is no time for mirth and laughter,
The cold gray dawn of the morning after.

I wanted to pay for ev'ry round;
I talked on subjects most profound;
When all my woes I analyzed,
The barkeep softly sympathized.
The world was one kaleidoscope
Of purple bliss, transcendent hope.
But now I'm feeling mighty blue—
Three cheers for the W. C. T. U.!
R–E–M–O–R–S–E!
Those dry Martinis did the work for me;
Last night at twelve I felt immense,
Today I feel like thirty cents.
My eyes are bleared, my coppers hot,
I'll try to eat, but I cannot.
It is no time for mirth and laughter,
The cold, gray dawn of the morning after.

George Ade (1866–1944)